TIM
KIPPER

Robert Swindells

Illustrated by Scoular Anderson

M
MACMILLAN CHILDREN'S BOOKS

First published 1990 by
MACMILLAN CHILDREN'S BOOKS
A division of Macmillan Publishers Limited
London and Basingstoke
Associated companies throughout the world

ISBN 0-333-51749-0

A CIP catalogue record for this book is available from the British Library.

Typeset by Universe Typesetters

Printed in Hong Kong

Tim Kipper was a silly man
Who thought that it was yummy
To swallow clouds of dirty smoke
Right down into his tummy.

And though it made him want to cough
As it was going down

He went on doing it, until

It turned his insides brown.

He'd say to everyone he met

'Hey –

have you got a light?'

He got through twenty smokes a day

And twenty-five at night.

Then, one morning, feeling odd,
He scrambled out of bed
And looking in the mirror
Saw a chimney on his head.

It was just a little chimney –
He could hide it with his hair –

But anyway, he sulked all day
And wished it wasn't there.

He tossed and turned in bed that night

His head felt rather sore.

And in the morning, you-know-what
Was taller than before.

(And if you're feeling worried

And your head is rather sore

You can't stop smoking cigarettes –

You want them more and more.)

'Oh, heck!' he cried. 'Oh, crikey –
What will the neighbours say?

I'll have to get myself a hat
And keep it on all day.'

He passed Miss Manning in the lane,
She murmured, 'Fancy that –
Tim Kipper must be feeling cold –
He's bought himself a hat.'

Poor Tim slept badly once again
And woke up feeling ill.
He felt his chimney with his hand
And it was taller still.

'This is no joke!' he cried. 'A smoke
Will calm me down a bit.'

And after that he fetched his hat –
And found it didn't fit.

'Oh, flippin' heck!' He scratched his neck.
'I really look a sight.
I'll put my grandad's topper on
And that'll hide it – right?'

But everybody pointed
As he scuttled to his car

'Lord Snooty's got his topper on,'
They chuckled, 'Ha, ha, ha!'

(And if you're being laughed at
And your chimney's growing tall

And you've got a hundred cigarettes
It makes you smoke them all.)

He slept upon the floor that night
(He couldn't fit in bed)
And next day he was forced to wear
The dustbin on his head.

He couldn't get inside the car
And so he had to walk.
He couldn't hear, he couldn't see —
He couldn't even talk.

The chimney grew, till it became
As tall as any tree.

'I cannot hide it any more,'
Said Tim. 'Oh, woe is me!'

The chimney grew so heavy now
That Tim could scarcely walk.
He went to see the doctor
And they had a little talk.

The doctor said, 'You're most unwell –
You've got a dreadful cough.
I'm sending you to hospital
To have that chimney off.'

So Tim went into hospital,
The nurse was very kind.
'You might be here a while,' she said,
And Tim said, 'I don't mind.'

She took his cigarettes away
And said, 'We'll make you fit,'
And he had an operation
And it only hurt a bit.

He really missed his cigarettes,
It made him quite downhearted.
And every day he'd groan and say,
'I wish I'd never started.'

A long time passed, and then at last
The nurse said, 'Home today –
But don't go back to smoking, Tim,'
And the patient said, 'No way.'

The nurse brought in a looking-glass
And Tim admired the view –
His head was like it used to be
Before his chimney grew.

Now Tim can race,

and fly through space

And lift a garden shed.

You'd never know he used to grow
A chimney on his head.